I0402539

Thriving in a World of Constant Change

Mini-Book Strategy Series – Book 7

Authors: Rand Morimoto, Ph.D.

Rich Dorfman, MBA

DEDICATION

I dedicate this book to my family: Ana, Noble, Kelly, Chip, and Eduardo
for making life special every day - Rand

I dedicate this book to my wife Sherry. Thanks Sherry for inspiring and
coaching me! - Rich

TABLE OF CONTENTS

Mini-Book Strategy Series – Book 7 i

Dedication...iii

Table of Contents v

Introduction...1

Chapter 1: Accelerated Change – What's Happening? 3

Global Marketplace 4

Rapid Delivery..4

Psychological Influence 5

Trend Manipulation..5

A Business Model Disruptive by Nature 5

Chapter 2: Is Tech to Blame?..7

Disruptive Changes Caused by Buyer Demands 7

Disruption Caused by a Disposable Products Environment.......8

Disruption Caused by Shifting Work Habits and Patterns 9

Tech – The Right Solution at the Right Time.........................9

Chapter 3: Buying Habits in the New Era 11

Housing Pricing 12

Rent versus Buy 12

Car Service versus Car Purchase 12

Long Days and Limited Hours...12

Shared Environment – Lower Demand for Individual Consumer Goods...13

Impact of Online Communications......................................13

Chapter 4: Avoiding the Impact of Perceptions and Downside Aspects of the Internet 15

Manipulation of Reality 16

Impact of Social Media..16

Loud Voice for Individuals 17

Impact of Instantaneous Information....................................18

Unspinning Inaccurate Information 18

Chapter 5: If You Can't Beat 'em, then Join 'em......................21

Velocity of Global Change 22

Cutting Out the Middleman..23

Establishing Product and Market Dominance......................23

Venture Capital Funding Lasts Longer than Organizations Can Stay Alive 24

Chapter 6: Lessons Learned from Transformations in the Fast-Paced Tech Industry...27
    Datacenters versus Cloud...28
    Shift in the Role of Technology Evolution Thinking.................28
    Differentiating One to Another..30
    Using Data as a Competitive Advantage 31
Chapter 7: The Shift from Academic Practice to New World Reality 33
    Role of the Chief Executive Officer (CEO) 35
    Role of the Chief Financial Officer (CFO) 35
    Head of Marketing and Sales 35
    Head of Human Resources (HR)..36
    Head of Operations..36
    Head of Legal, Security, Compliance, and Risk Management....36
    New World of Business – New Thinking in Business Management 37
Chapter 8: The Path Forward 39
    Be Aware and Well Informed...39
    Be Fast and Nimble...40
    Diversify...40
    Broad Set Profitability...41
    Innovate with Passion...41
    Assess Employee Change 42
    Contracting for Change 43
    Enabling Technology to Solve Business Challenges...................43
    Leveraging Data Analytics to be Fully Informed 44
    Wrap-Up 44
MINI-BOOK STRATEGY SERIES 45
    New World of I.T..45
    Cybersecurity: Being Cyber Aware and Cyber Safe...................45
    Handling Electronically Stored Information (ESI) in the Era of the Cloud..46
    Application and Datacenter Modernization 46
    Adapting to the New World of I.T...47
    Shifting I.T. from Technologies to a Business Services Enabler 47
ABOUT THE AUTHORS 49

INTRODUCTION

Living in a world where technology is changing everything around us, the rapid advances and uses of technology over the past decade have completely upended how organizations use (or are impacted) by technology. Unlike just a decade ago where tech merely meant basic email, file sharing, and data entry, these days the proper use of technologies drive competitive advantages for organizations enabling enterprises to reach customers, predict trends, and transact in ways never possible before these new technologies were available.

The accelerated model of technological change has bled into the business models of non-tech industries including manufacturing, retail, finance, healthcare, and the like.

Organizations that used to do 5-10-year planning on their use of technology are realizing they need to do 3-5-year planning or even shorter cycles because competitors in their industry are taking first mover positions and completely disrupting the traditional flow of business operations in their industry.

The workforce that our parents or grandparents grew up in saw a shift from a lifetime career in one organization to a model where one might shift careers or organizations several times in a life span, where entrants in the workforce have no expectations of remaining at the same company, and potentially even in the same industry for more than a few years.

Lessons have been learned in industries that have already gone through this transformation from steady state businesses to those of managed chaos. There are many casualties in recent past and many more in sight (brick and mortar retail giving way to online retailers; grocery industry being gobbled up by tech; travel agents replaced by online travel sites; music and entertainment establishments being replaced by streaming and online services; the list goes on).

This book covers the changes that have gone on over the past few years, and provides real world examples for what organizations have done (and others can do) to not be a victim of tech, but leverage the new opportunities available in this new world of constant change.

CHAPTER 1: ACCELERATED CHANGE – WHAT'S HAPPENING?

Just a decade or two ago, life was pretty predictable. Employees would clock in and clock out each day doing, for the most part, the same thing they did a day, week, year ago. Automakers would show off their new line of cars in the summer, a new season of TV programming would come out in the Fall, every 3-5 years something slightly new or different was released that was marginally exciting, but for the most part, life was routine.

In the past dozen years, major anchor stores like Sears and JCPenney were going out of business, Blockbuster movie rental stores fell off the face of the earth, and automakers stopped selling entire lines of cars they've been selling for decades. Much that "used to be" is gone and different in just a few short years. What Happened???

Global Marketplace

One of the key factors in the rapid changes of the past decade has been the impact of the global marketplace, not just in commerce. Today, we live in a world where communications and people's awareness of current events has been accelerated from daily newspapers, to twice daily TV news, to online website, to one-line news feeds (like Twitter) having instantaneous global information pushed 24x7 right to mobile phones in real time.

The marketplace today extends what used to be the power of a local seller marketing to their community through localized advertising to now sellers reaching customers worldwide. However, with consumers connected to applications and devices in their pockets with information flowing to them from anywhere in the world, those disseminating information can reach millions and billions of potential buyers, completely changing the economics of small local sellers to large high volume, low margin, mass market enterprises.

Rapid Delivery

Another major influencing factor on buying decisions has been the ability for the large mass marketers to deliver their products in 2-days, 1-day, or even same day. While it used to be beneficial to go to a local store on the weekend to buy something since it was faster than waiting 1-2 weeks for a package to arrive by mail, consumers can click and buy something and have it delivered right to their doorstep before the weekend arrives and without the need to fight traffic, parking, or crowds at the mall.

A local retailer's weekend sale advertised through a local print or billboard ad is usurped by a global seller promoting something new, different, or trendy that'll be delivered to the buyer's door the next day with free shipping. Rapid door to door delivery has drastically changed the buying habits of consumers and has made it difficult for local retailers to buy and stock "today's trendy item" that just showed up as the cool thing to buy on Instagram just a few days prior.

Psychological Influence

Instant access to information from anywhere in the world has influenced trends, buying patterns, social interests, travel interests, and political ideals with many of the savviest influencers leveraging psychological methods to invoke emotions to persuade, convince, and manipulate individuals around the globe. Information disseminated over the Internet or through social media does not go through filters or validation of accuracy of information. Entire scenes and scenarios can be made up, captured on video, and distributed worldwide in seconds with the result of manipulating the belief of others that something is actually happening, when in reality, it may just be fabricated for the purpose of invoking fear, hate, interest, or desire.

Social media influencers are frequently being caught Photoshopping images that builds a perception that everyone should look a certain way, or that everyone should be traveling to certain places, or that everyone's reality should mirror an edited, Photoshopped, or staged environment.

Trend Manipulation

With access to millions and billions of consumers 24x7, the savvy sellers can identify what they are over stocked in and want to quickly sell. By manipulating buying trends, they can "create" interest and buzz on social media, build an artificial frenzy of interest in an item, and then push out ads to deliver such items overnight directly to the buyer. With a global marketplace, instant communications, the ability to manipulate consumers through social and online media, and next day delivery, those who know how to "work the system" have a much greater advantage over those who don't.

A Business Model Disruptive by Nature

Not all changes are deceptive or manipulative in intent, in fact industry or marketplace disruption has happened for decades with the rise of industrialization that shifted workers from farmland to cities, the shift to Henry Ford's model of production line manufacturing over custom development, or the shift to air travel over steam liners. Even prior to the past century, going back through history and time, there's been shifts from bow and arrow to guns, the introduction of indoor plumbing replacing chamber pots, and even the shift to farming from being hunters and gatherers. Change has always happened.

Business model disruption is what has advanced society for centuries. The biggest difference is the change in the past decade has been rapid and widespread, with market disruption happening in months and years, not over decades of time. Changes in the past tended to be isolated to a specific market or region that took years or decades to trickle around the globe, that now happen instantaneously worldwide. For those in one of these disrupting businesses, the accelerated change is the basis of their business. For those competing against one of these disrupting businesses, the leadership team of those organizations must change their business model to be competitive.

With rapid global changes, organizations don't have the luxury of sampling something in a test market or developing a traditional 3, 5, and 10-year business plan for change and transition. Business leaders are having to jump in with both feet and start being innovative, competitive, and disruptive themselves to survive.

CHAPTER 2: IS TECH TO BLAME?

No doubt, technology has impacted industries like music and movie rentals as streaming media was facilitated through the Internet, and technology has made consumer buying easier with a click of a button than by "ordering by phone" in the mail order catalog days of the 1980s and 1990s or driving to the mall or shopping center before that.

Disruptive Changes Caused by Buyer Demands

However, in early 2019, both Ford Motor Co. and Volkswagen started the process of eliminating what used to be "bread and butter" selling sedans, as American auto buyer's demand shifted toward crossover sports utility vehicles (SUVs) with buyers interested in more cargo space, more legroom for passengers, and a more luxurious ride and experience. (https://www.cnet.com/roadshow/news/volkswagen-beetle-final-assembly/)

These changes aren't tech things, it's the globalization of automobile buying interests and the differentiation between various auto brands that makes it harder for businesses to "own" certain regional markets or certain segments or classes of products when they are now competing against sellers around the globe. What differentiated cars a decade ago (safety records, cruise control, leather seats, and audio system) have become standard across models. There's very little product feature differentiation between one 4 door sedan and another.

Disruption Caused by a Disposable Products Environment

Consumer purchases across a wide range of products have become disposable by nature, whether that's one-time use water and soda bottles, plastic bags, plastic encased consumer items, fast food containers, or even disposable mobile phones. Consumers buy products that they use once and throw away. Consumers buy products in containers, wrapped in a bag, and shipped in a box where all of the outer shipping and delivery materials are thrown away. Even entire consumer product devices are deemed disposable if they stop working after their perceived useful life is up.

Consumer product purchases in the United States once dominated by U.S. and Japanese manufacturers like RCA, Sony, Westinghouse, Texas Instruments, and Kenmore have been greatly impacted from global marketing, shipping, delivery, and support with companies like Samsung, Huawei, and LG. As consumers buy more products online, they have less of an expectation that they can walk into a store to get the product repaired. No longer is a relationship formed with a store front retailer, and thus the requirement to have service centers coast to coast is no longer a barrier to entry by a manufacturer, distributor, or seller into serving a marketplace. This has allowed companies to enter markets with no real plan or method of supporting or servicing their product(s) in that marketplace. For many products these days, they have a useful life of just 12-24 months. So, when the product breaks, the buyer just throws the item away (or hopefully puts it in a recycle bin or drops it off at an eWaste site); and the consumer goes out and purchases a new item.

Disruption Caused by Shifting Work Habits and Patterns

In 2018 when McDonalds shifted from frozen meat patties to fresh meat patties, their sale of Quarter Pounders increased by 30%. McDonalds changed their product to meet the buyer demand of ingredient transparency. (https://www.cnn.com/2019/06/24/business/mcdonalds-fresh-beef/index.html) Consumers have shifted to buying more foods and services from others because of a change in more solitary households (younger generation not getting married and starting a family early on) or as a result of dual income households (both spouses working full time).

Unlike years past when a household had a stay-at-home spouse, typically the wife, who had time to go to the market, go to the shopping mall, and do things while the kids were away at school. However, with more women choosing to enter and stay in the workforce, there's less time and interest to go to the mall, wait in line at the market, or even spend an hour a day preparing a meal. This shift in lifestyle over the past couple of decades has driven consumers to accept services that help them maximize their time in a day. Instead of driving store to store to find something, being able to order through an application and have it delivered in the next day or two proved to be the right service at the right time for a buyer's evolving needs.

Tech – The Right Solution at the Right Time

Here's a "chicken and the egg" question, did tech drive people to buy this new way, or did lifestyles changes over the past 20 to 30 years drive a services economy as the right solution to fulfill on changing market demands? Whatever the answer may be, when busy consumers were able to click a button on their mobile device in their pocket or purse to quickly order what they want and receive it the next day (or same day!), tech flourished and benefited from this opportunity.

- The Internet with the World Wide Web, rolled out in the mid-1990s to the public, provided a universal platform for communications and global information access and data transmission to every part of the world.
- Mobile devices rolled out in the mid-2000s put a device in consumer's pockets and purses that brought information from the Internet right to consumer's fingertips when they were at work, at home, or virtually anywhere.
- Mobile apps made it simple for users to quickly search, find, and buy products with a tap of a finger to buy whatever they wanted, at any time, from anywhere.
- Review websites helped buyers research what item, which store (or online store), and the right price of the item that is desired to be purchased.
- Express shipping enabled organizations to have products delivered within 2-days, 1-day, or even same day to consumers, minimizing the gap from the time someone wanted something to the time they had it in their hands.
- Social media accelerated the influence of sellers to spark demand and extend the awareness of products to consumers.

The last four bullet points in the above list have only been on the scene for the past decade. Tech no doubt took advantage of an awaiting market demand for busy, mobile, and global consumers over the past 25-years. And in the past decade, all of the pieces needed to put the "icing on the cake" were rolled out in a way that has made the global marketplace more accessible, to more people, to reach more buyers, instantaneously, 24-hours a day, 7-days a week.

CHAPTER 3: BUYING HABITS IN THE NEW ERA

Millennials are frequently blamed as being the drivers of the services industry, choosing to use ride services like Uber and Lyft instead of buying cars, renting instead of buying houses, or going out to eat instead of preparing their own meals at home. However, anyone with family or friends in their 40s and 50s with young kids, living in big houses, with both parents working full time jobs, driving electric vehicles, can see where the boomers, Gen-X, and Gen-Ys are driving the purchase of disposal products and the service-driven industry as well.

While the Millennials may be a generation that as a whole are heavily participating in the current services economy, as noted in the previous chapter "Is Tech to Blame?", it's neither tech nor a particular generation of individuals causing this rapid change in market dynamics and economics.

When one stops and looks around, there are MANY factors that drive the "chicken or the egg" question, is change in demand growing the services industry, or is the services industry driving this change in consumer habits? It's all part of this ongoing market economy that we're living in.

Housing Pricing

Worse in major metropolitan areas, but the same situation globally, the cost of housing has skyrocketed to the point where the work force is required to pay a lot on mortgage payments or rent to live close to where they work. As an alternative, they can still pay a lot, but usually a more manageable budget amount to live 30, 60, even 90 minutes away from their jobs. This holds true for cities around the world including San Francisco, Los Angeles, Dallas, Chicago, New York, London, Paris, Beijing, Tokyo, Singapore, and Sydney.

Rent versus Buy

Many in the work force choose to not spend 1-2 hours each way each day on their commute to work and thus elect to rent an apartment or a room in a house to be closer to where they work. Renting is not a decision born by not "wanting" to buy a house, but rather the pure economics of not being able to afford to buy in a community within a reasonable commute distance to work.

Car Service versus Car Purchase

With traffic being so bad in big cities, and the cost of parking being so expensive, it's not always a choice whether one hails a driving service like Uber and Lyft as opposed to owning, driving, and finding a place to park a vehicle. And many modern cities don't have an adequate public transportation system, or the places where businesses have chosen to place their businesses are not in convenient places where public transportation is available. When there's no place to park and public transportation doesn't bring you near your destination, using ride hailing services fills that gap.

Long Days and Limited Hours

Income levels needed to pay for expensive mortgages and rents require workers spend more hours on the job to make ends meet.

Long commutes to work make days longer, so the last thing the modern worker wants to do is get home and start preparing dinner. For many, apartments may be much smaller or even shared with roommates, so it can be harder to prepare meals in limited or even shared spaces. This all leads the working consumers to eat out more often or use food delivery services like DoorDash than to find time to shop, cook, and eat in the living conditions they're in.

Shared Environment – Lower Demand for Individual Consumer Goods

As more of the workforce lives in a shared environment through renting or shared living arrangements, this diminishes the need for each individual to have (or need) their own washer and dryer, refrigerator, and car. Those living in apartments or shared living spaces may share laundry services across 20 or 30 people. Multiple people living in a same house or apartment won't have space for multiple vehicles to park at night, thus less of an opportunity to have multiple cars. All these elements contribute to a clear shift from goods to services.

When an apartment complex has a shared laundry room, it may be more convenient to just send laundry out to a laundry service than to spend an entire morning or evening waiting for a shared washing machine and dryer to become available. Shared space typically has limited gardening space, and busy individuals have limited time to do gardening, so instead of growing fresh fruits and vegetables, it is more convenient to buy organics at the market or through online delivery services, thus enforcing a "buy" versus a "grow" model of daily goods.

Impact of Online Communications

Do Facebook (FB) and Instagram (IG) replace our need to keep up face to face contact with family and friends, or are our lives so busy that we don't have as many hours to meet up with people after work or on weekends and thus FB and IG are a good alternative? For many, if it weren't for online communications (Skype, Facebook, etc.), it could be years before someone would see another family member or friend at a wedding or funeral. However, for others, the online communications have become the excuse why going out of the way to meet up with someone for dinner, for a weekend, or even as a vacation destination is no longer needed.

Online communications has changed the way people interact, feeling they are "in touch" with others when it may have been years or decades since they actually physically met up in person, spent time with someone, and shared more than just the online posted picture highlights of day to day living.

CHAPTER 4: AVOIDING THE IMPACT OF PERCEPTIONS AND DOWNSIDE ASPECTS OF THE INTERNET

The tech industry has no doubt been directly involved in the disruptive market environment. It could be argued either way - that tech is good, or tech is bad, as it relates to the current economic, sociological, and political environments. There are real impacts caused by tech as already covered in this book on tech's impact on retail sales, globalization of sales and the market economy. However, tech has also changed business and operational dynamics with impacts caused by perceptions, manipulations, social and societal impacts.

While these impacts are real, whether they are a bad thing or could be used for common good is solely dependent on how technologies are used and the personal filter individuals put on everything they read and see on the Internet, to blindly accept versus taking a critical eye on whether perception is really reality.

Manipulation of Reality

As has been shared earlier in this book, pictures found on the internet are sometimes Photoshopped. And, just because someone writes something on the Internet, it doesn't mean it is true and accurate. Information on the Internet is solely shared "raw" content and individual opinions.

As with any argument, there's always two (or more) sides to the argument, and there are often times two (or more) interpretations of the exact same information. Start with the belief that what you are reading and seeing is purely a singular perspective of a single individual. Even as others repost the same picture with additional input and comments, most of the time those reposting and adding in comments are not firsthand participants that "are there" seeing things with their own eyes, or actively participating in the activities going on.

Many individuals posting, reposting, and commenting on information on the Internet do so solely to share false information, manipulate others, and do so for satirical reasons. In these cases, there is rarely any truth to their posting and comments, and thus those participating on the Internet should be aware that what they are reading and seeing could very well be far from the truth and reality.

Organizations need to be aware that the anonymous nature of the Internet allows for the open sharing of false and manipulative information; and the organization should be prepared to diffuse improper, insensitive, or inaccurate information. Many times, "fact checking" individual posts will redirect readers from an opinion to a link with real information, formally clarifying what's fact vs. what's opinion. The ability to moderate posts on sites the organization can control and working with the source organizations to have content moderated on their sites give an organization the ability to have inaccurate or socially irresponsible information removed.

Impact of Social Media

Because of the relatively anonymous platform that social media provides, where those who post or comment on information do not have to prove their identity to get an account, participants can post whatever they want without regard to normal social norms of politeness and respect.

It has become a sport for many to refute, rebuke, and bully others with no recourse. Social media can be emotionally uplifting for those who do it for the "likes". However, with limited filters and no mediation from bad actors, social media can be very demoralizing for many, even causing emotional pain and depression.

Organizations need to prevent bullies from creating online fights and spats on an organization's social media (or other related accounts) that are detrimental to the proper communications by most people. Raising the expectation of communications on social media to the level one would expect in face to face communications in a respectable business environment sets the bar such that the anonymous nature of the Internet doesn't give some participants an open forum to communicate in an inappropriate manner.

Loud Voice for Individuals

Since social media has limited filters, it gives some individuals a louder voice than what they might otherwise be provided in other settings. This raises the power of a bully or any individual by elevating the voice of one over the voice of others.

Through the user of bots and the ability for an individual to create as many accounts as they want, an individual can drown out the voices of others merely by automating responses either for or against a topic or viewpoint, skewing the voice of reality from that of a well tooled individual.

Organizations need to be savvy enough to see through smear campaigns instigated by disgruntled individuals or even competitors seeking to leverage the Internet to cause harm to an organization. As vocal as some individuals could be in trying to influence the dialog and perception against an organization, executives need to use the same tactics to their benefit by having counter tactics on social media to balance the influence of "bad actors".

Impact of Instantaneous Information

In an era when the "news" broke with the release of the morning newspaper, there was time during the day or evening to assess a situation after hours of gathered information, verified facts, and "full reporting" of a situation with background on the potential cause, impact, and current status.

However, in a world where individuals report on a breaking situation with pictures and opinions, the first set of "facts" may very well be completely wrong, solely taken from the words of one individual, not verifying the actual facts nor validating the situation at hand.

Global and societal awareness of an unfolding event is purely the conjecture of what "appears to be happening" from the limited first line sources. The other 99% of information tend to be posts, reposts, and interpretations from others. It's like the old game of "telephone" where one person says something, passes that on to the next person, who passes it on to the next person, and so forth with the final message being NOTHING like what was said in the first place. And in the case of situational reporting, that even presumes the first message was even accurate and real. The story is told before the facts are in, which should make instantaneous information distribution believed to only be an opinion and representative of the partial facts that it really is.

Of course, organizations cannot control every "first post" out on the Internet. Organizations can proactively post information to start conversations, disclose information, or factually respond to information posted on the Internet so as to influence the dialog in a manner appropriate and responsible for the organization.

Unspinning Inaccurate Information

Unfortunately, on the Internet, it is difficult to unpost and undo something once it is published. Information on the Internet is difficult to erase; and once harm is done, it is nearly impossible to undo it. This is why it's potentially dangerous to believe everything you hear and read on the Internet as fact until you have an opportunity to validate the facts and confirm what you heard and read is truly accurate.

Enterprises leveraging social media and external Internet communications must be prepared to balance quick, immediate actions and responses to "keep up with Internet speed", while ensuring communications are accurate and factual. It's better to be slightly delayed but accurate, than first out and being factually wrong, as the impact can be devasting for organizations proven to be false that can take much more time and costs to repair things after the fact.

CHAPTER 4: AVOIDING THE IMPACT OF PERCEPTIONS AND DOWNSIDE ASPECTS OF THE INTERNET

CHAPTER 5: IF YOU CAN'T BEAT 'EM, THEN JOIN 'EM

With all the potential risks that come from the challenges of adopting a new or different business model, the fast-paced services economy isn't just a fad, it's here to stay. One can sit on the sideline and complain about the change or choose to embrace the change, especially when the global services economy model is well engrained in the day to day lifestyle of consumers today. Even for organizations that don't provide a consumer product or a direct to consumer service, the enterprise workforce is participating in this new lifestyle and way of living. And, the employer needs to adapt its human resources and personnel support processes to accommodate its employees.

At a minimum, the enterprise needs to ensure that it is conscientiously assessing and creatively developing new ways to run its operations to address the globalization of buyers, sellers, workers, information, communications, security, compliance, politics, and sociological sentiment.

Velocity of Global Change

Perhaps the biggest factor in the changes going on in the current global market environment is that not only is change happening, but the velocity of the change is putting successful organizations out of business faster than they can write their 5 and 10-year business plans. As stated earlier in this book, the mobile phone and "apps" on phones has only been around for just a decade. In 10 short years, there's been incredible speed to which consumers, employees, and families from around the globe have changed and adjusted to a model of instant global information access, instantaneous purchase ability, and direct influence from traditional advertisers, including some with nefarious intent.

Today, when you're too far behind, you risk not being able to catch up quickly enough to survive. And, the larger the enterprise, the harder it is to be nimble enough to make the changes necessary to adapt to the new world environment.

Take an organization like Blockbuster movie rentals, an organization that reached over 9000 stores in 2004 successfully renting video DVDs to consumers every night of the week. However, within 6-years, Blockbuster had filed for bankruptcy protection as DVDs shipped by mail from a consumer services organization (Netflix) made it more convenient for consumers to get the video they wanted delivered right to their door without having to walk into a store to find the title unavailable.

Blockbuster didn't even survive long enough to face the full online streaming model that has taken place within the past decade where thousands of movie titles are now available at a touch of a button to stream over the internet. In a short 10-years, the "movie rental" business had at least two drastic changes in its business model.

And now a third transition is taking place as Disney+ is changing that industry once again by removing all Disney and its associated properties (Pixar, Marvel Studios, Star Wars, and 20th Century Fox) from streaming content providers and will be competing head to head with these providers. Third party streaming content providers just like cable television providers are and will be facing the challenge of competing against the production studios and content copyright holders themselves as the barrier to entry into streaming content to reaching millions of paying consumers has created a drastic change in the business environment.

Cutting Out the Middleman

No longer do manufacturers, producers, and traditional "behind the scenes" providers have to go through layers and layers of middlemen to get to the consumer. The concept of farm to table is more than just providing organic foods directly to the consumer; but it's the change that internet-based selling, global rapid shipping and delivery, and consumers with a services economy mindset benefit from buying directly from the producer.

The benefit the consumer gets may be in lower prices. In some cases the consumer pays even MORE than what they would normally pay through multiple layers of distributors and retailers, where the end buyer feels they are getting something fresher (shorter shipping and delivery times), helping the producer (directly help the little guy who is putting in the labor to produce the goods), or simply rebelling against the large corporate middlemen.

Just a couple decades ago, it did take these middlemen to buy, process, and transport goods in bulk to bring them to consumers with a relatively low mark-up. However, with the changes in Internet marketing and the ability to find transportation brokers with a touch of a button to arrange shipping and delivery, the processing and transportation of goods is no longer a complex mystery.

Establishing Product and Market Dominance

A few decades ago, establishing product and market dominance meant being the anchor store or being near the anchor store in a shopping mall, something that the retailer Sears did for years. However, even before the era of online shopping and next day shipping of good and services, Sears lost its edge in the higher end marketplace to Nordstrom, Neiman Marcus, and other retailers branded to the perception of higher quality goods. At the same time, Sears lost its edge against low cost retailers like Walmart and Target that sold everything Sears did plus grocery items and other day to day goods making other retailers a true one stop shop.

Nordstrom's, Neiman Marcus, Target, and Walmart beat Sears at its own game, by creating dominance in marketing of consumer goods that chipped away at Sears' ability to compete on the high end as well as on the low end, getting the squeeze and ultimately forcing Sears into bankruptcy protection. Just like in the Blockbuster store example, Sears stayed competitive in its retail store operation, but as Internet goods providers like Amazon rose to dominance selling and delivering products in 2-days, 1-day, or same day, Sears wasn't ready to compete against what was directly ahead of them.

Again, in a span of less than 15-years, the market environment changed twice, and Sears was caught flat footed and unable to react fast enough to compete with in the fast-paced changes going on around them. By the time Sears' management and Board realized they were behind, it was too late.

Venture Capital Funding Lasts Longer than Organizations Can Stay Alive

In the old days when a competitor up the street lowered their prices to win business, you knew they couldn't do that forever and at some point, they'd have to raise their prices, so you could always just wait them out. However, venture funded disrupters can run years and seemingly "forever" without making a profit, all funded through venture capital or through stock market funding.

The taxicab industry is one that has been facing competitive pressure from services like Uber and Lyft that haven't shown a profit since their inception, with many analysts wondering if the ride sharing industry can ever be profitable.

https://www.forbes.com/sites/lensherman/2019/06/02/can-uber-ever-be-profitable

How can taxicab businesses compete when a market disrupter is running its operation without business profitability for years? THIS is what organizations in all industries have to face, is a somewhat unfair advantage others have in running their operations, disrupting a business model, and doing so without the ability to attain and sustain being profitable.

CHAPTER 5: IF YOU CAN'T BEAT 'EM, THEN JOIN 'EM

CHAPTER 6: LESSONS LEARNED FROM TRANSFORMATIONS IN THE FAST-PACED TECH INDUSTRY

Analyzing the changes that have gone on in the fast-paced tech industry is frequently used in helping organizations understand the impact of change in the non-tech industry. With advances in tech (such as global real time Internet communications) being a major contributing factor in global market change over the past two decades, the tech industry and technologies themselves have evolved 2, 3, 4 times in that same period.

One of the key understandings that comes early in the analysis and assessment of change in the tech industry has been that the path forward looks nothing like the path the organization had taken to date. Any policy, process, best practices, competitive advantage, standard, and procedure that is older than 3-years old is likely not applicable for the organization moving forward.

While people and processes need to "continue" for a short period of time while the organization continues to maintain and manage existing systems and processes, it is a short lived expectation of "old ways of doing things" as the organization builds, implements, and operates in "new ways" as the enterprise moves forward.

Datacenters versus Cloud

For years, organizations built and managed their own datacenters and ran technology operations internally. Organizations got really good at operating their systems, minimizing downtime, and managing their security and business operations in a reliable and dependable manner. However as management steps back and looks at the cost to maintain and manage their own operations, with cloud services providing identical services at a much lower cost, it's not only a cost factor of shifting to the cloud, but a clear decision that unless the organization is in business to RUN I.T. operations, it is better off buying I.T. services (in the cloud) than spending the time and resources focusing on providing email, file sharing, telephony, web conferencing, and basic business applications on their own.

Organizations don't need to move 100% of their operations to the cloud, but even shifting 50%, 60%, 70% of the basic I.T. services to the cloud allows I.T. operations to focus on the business "apps" and leverage ways technology can be utilized to help the organization analyze data, leverage data, and take advantage of technology as a competitive business advantage.

Shift in the Role of Technology Evolution Thinking

As organizations shift from building, managing, and maintaining their own technology datacenters, the personnel in I.T. can be shifted from individuals doing mundane technical tasks, to being technology professionals that help the business units within the organization (sales, marketing, manufacturing, production, research & development, engineering, etc.) understand and use technology to help them to be more productive and do their jobs better.

Many of those in the workforce grew up doing things in older, manual, non-technology ways. Newer competitors that are building their businesses with a workforce that knows how to leverage technologies will gain a competitive advantage over organizations that have lagged behind. As much as "change" can be difficult for employees in an organization, and management may not want to "teach an old dog a new trick," whether the organization retools the knowledge of existing employees, or adds new employees with new skillsets, the management in the organization cannot sit back and say what it "can't do" but understand and realize that it might have to change to remain competitive in the fast paced disruptive global market that the world economy has become.

In the tech industry, it has been the change of adopting and adapting day to day processes to utilize new cloud-based technologies, embracing "continuous development" and "continuous upgrades" where technologies aren't updated every 3-5 years, but now part of a rolling update process where things are updated every 6-12 months, or even sooner.

These changes have started with the awareness of the new technological solutions by the personnel running and administering the environments, their learning of the new ways of doing things, and then implementing the new ways of doing things through their enterprises. The changes have been cultural changes in the mindset and practices leveraged by personnel to do things that are very different than what they've been doing for years.

Initially, there was hesitation in "changing" what has been successful in the organization for years, where I.T.'s contribution to their organization has been providing a reliable, stable, and dependable technology environment. Changing the ways things are done can disrupt that success and cause all of the things that I.T. deems as their value to break and change.

Even the senior-most executives in an organization that expect I.T. stability and reliability tend to have the latest and greatest phones, tablets, and gadgets, and are usually among the first to "update" their devices to take advantage of new features and functions released to the marketplace. Applying that same concept to their laptop and desktop computers and organizational backend computer systems, these same senior executives can see the value to being a nimble business on technologies that support the velocity of the business model the enterprise requires rather than lagging "behind" by 3, 5, 7, 10 years or more.

Differentiating One to Another

When innovation hits a plateau, how does one differentiate itself from another? This was one of the key drivers that ultimately changed the thinking in tech to stop doing the same thing it has always done and start doing things that were new, different, that felt uncomfortable, to break away from what everyone was used to. The change is what allowed the organization to differentiate itself from others and allowed the organization to create a strategic advantage.

For architectural and design firms that have for years used drafting boards for design creation and likely shifted to Computer Aided Design (CAD) software to two-dimensional and even three-dimensional designs, there have been distinct changes in the use of technology to "visualize" three-dimensional concepts using 3D goggles and multi-dimensional displays. Organizations can continue to do things the way "it has always done". These same organizations will be seriously threatened by entrants to the market and industry that can do all of the old ways of doing things plus new ways. This sparks interest and entices customers who perceive this company to be smarter, more innovative, cutting edge, and unique, and has proven to be enough for new entrants to get a foothold into a marketplace and industry through differentiating from others.

Technology has been leveraged by product sellers by having applications and mobile apps that provide their customers real time inventory data, access to view available products and services, ability to buy and transact services with a touch of a button, and the ability to track shipments and deliveries. For many organizations, all of this has been available "just a phone call away" where someone can call and get updates. However, buyers have seen what they could do on their consumer side purchases tracking items they order from

Amazon, Apple, Uber and DoorDash, such that they have an expectation that their business to business transactions have the same ease of information look-up and rich real time data access as their day to day consumer-based transactions.

Consumer services have set a level of expectations that when a business person has to "make a phone call" or "wait for someone to get back to them with information," the businesses that can provide similar information services business to business will have a technological competitive edge over other organizations. Despite a business being successful for years, its future success is threatened by these newer entrants that provide consumer level data information and access, differentiating themselves as being more innovative and responsive to their customers.

Using Data as a Competitive Advantage

There have been many organizations that have leveraged their ability to utilize "data" to be their competitive advantage. For many organizations, knowing who bought what, when, and how many, was merely a tool to "look backwards" into historical transactions. However, those who can take historical data and look forward into potential future behavior is leveraging the benefits of predictive analytics, that helps organizations better manage employee and customer behavior.

Taking the example of a customer that has historically bought items at the end of every quarter, knowing that, an organization can use that datapoint to proactively contact the customer toward the end of the quarter to start the process of lining up the next order. Rather than waiting 2-3 months or even longer to wonder why a customer stopped buying from them, only to realize the customer went elsewhere months ago, the strategy of contacting a customer ahead of time allows the organization to realize in real-time that maybe their costs need to be adjusted or the customer's buying needs have changed and allow the organization to adapt its pricing or offering to retain the customer.

If the data suggests that a customer always buys the latest and greatest item as soon as it is available, an organization can make that customer aware of an upcoming release of an item and take a pre-order before the customer can find the item elsewhere.

For organizations that manufacture products, they can review historical data and determine when peak buying periods are, and ramp up sales for the peak period and scale back production in slower times. Rather than filling warehouses with product, an organization can manage their inventory better based on actual analysis of historical data.

Analyzing data doesn't need to be limited to internal organizational information but can be extended to external information. Understanding market trends, regional trends, how weather and seasonal variances, local transportation data, as well as other employee behavior and experiences can impact decision making and enable an organization to better respond, react, and support its employees and its customers.

CHAPTER 7: THE SHIFT FROM ACADEMIC
PRACTICE TO NEW WORLD REALITY

The global marketplace today is different than it was just a decade ago, and there's little indication that the world will revert back to the way things were before. The forces of market disruption are made even more complex with the entry of new competitors willing to forego profits and use social media to "manipulate reality" to influence an existing market or to make a new market. This is a challenging time for executives with years of real-world experience supplemented with academic learning (MBA degrees) familiar with the way things "have always been." But the economics going on today is unlike anything that was taught in school or that executives have experienced over the past century.

Executives are getting caught flat footed and are ill prepared to tackle this new way of business. With these trends likely to continue for the foreseeable future, they have the choice to either let it happen around them, or rethink how business is done today to be able to thrive in the changing business environment. Historically, executives could at least plan on competitors being motivated by profitability and ideas that made "business sense"; however, today, executives need to rethink its business model to account for these new, somewhat illogical forces that have appeared.

For forward thinking professionals, it can be an exciting time with lots of opportunity for innovation, developing new ways of doing things, what it means to being in a first mover position and leading the marketplace and industry. And, whether an organization is focused on consumers or businesses, executives can learn from consumer-focused examples such as the on-demand movies example, as they provide powerful and insightful views into this New World of constant and rapid change.

These changes fundamentally impact every important function in the business, so whether one focuses on business strategy, financial controls, sales and marketing, operations or security, compliance, pr risk management, the executive needs to think differently, act differently and go beyond what professional training and experience has taught them. For those of us who have completed our formal education more than a decade ago and have leveraged what we learned to achieve success, principles like the value of long-term planning, treating employees fairly so they would be loyal, long term contributors, and using traditional business models have found what worked before doesn't work the same today.

Several variables affect success: strategic thinking, corporate policies, business process automation, best practices & tools and technology to name a few. Next, we'll take a high-level look by business function. Putting on the various hats we wear in leadership roles for our business, here are the major impact areas to think about and plan for.

Role of the Chief Executive Officer (CEO)

As CEO, we need to focus on our current business model, ensuring it is successful today and forecast to be successful for the next year or more and that our value proposition for our customers is unique and maintainable. As we look at threats, we need to know if any competitor is lurking on the horizon exhibiting signs of having a competitive focus. We need to be researching social media sites frequently and networking with peers to proactively look out for "false realities". And, if after all this, we feel good about where we are and the lack of threats lurking, we need to be looking for opportunities for expansion and for diversification. A best practice recommendation is to monitor all these factors at least monthly, so we factor in the rapid pace of change around us.

Role of the Chief Financial Officer (CFO)

As CFO, we need to adjust our focus and speed to match the rapid changes we're seeing. From a revenue and profitability perspective, some of the biggest challenges come from adapting to a world of predictive analytics and forecasting versus relying on historical data and leveraging readily available external information. From a cost management standpoint, we need to review and be ready to adjust all cost categories from buying and owning to outsourcing and renting, be it capital items or people, be it facilities or business functions (such as IT). And, we need to review and assess vendor and supplier relationships to ensure we're optimizing spend, margins, and in some cases, even the necessity of the relationship.

Head of Marketing and Sales

As head of Marketing and Sales, we can still leverage the classic 4 P's of Marketing (price, product, promotion, and place) per the classic Proctor and Gamble retail consumer model we learned in school to assess our target market, look at current shopping and buying habits, assess the threats posed by current and upcoming competitors, to gauge how that affects pricing, advertising, and selling activities. Broadly speaking, we can expect our buyers to be increasingly more sophisticated, more knowledgeable, and more demanding, challenging our marketing and our selling to evolve in order to meet our revenue / profit targets.

Head of Human Resources (HR)

As head of HR, we need to understand that today's "modern workforce" requires a totally different mindset than 10-15 years ago, that to successfully attract and retain talented people will require more than just an attractive compensation and benefits package, but also needs to include a culture of growth mindset and attention on people. Despite advances in technology that make digital communications easier, frequent face-face employee connections are important, as is the ability to offer employees flexible, personalized arrangements. Some employees will need to be challenged, others will need to see a clear path for advancement, and still others will value work-life balance and freedom of where they work and how much they work.

Head of Operations

As head of Operations, we need to assess internal business processes as well as any applicable external functions such as distribution, delivery, supply chain, and logistics to identify any that are sub-optimal. From this assessment, a gap analysis and action plan can be developed that works towards optimizing operational efficiency and cost-effectiveness.

Head of Legal, Compliance, Risk Management, and Security

For those leaders responsible for Legal, Security, Compliance, and Risk Management, responsibilities have grown and gotten a lot more complex as security threats and compliance requirement continue to evolve. In particular, information protection requirements have dramatically evolved. As a starting point, we must be aware of new requirements. Next, we must examine existing policies, as many organizations have policies that were designed for the past and don't apply / aren't optimized for the New World we're in. As we move more towards outsourcing, be it business functions like IT or even people, using more contractors in place of employees, we need to review and adapt policies and processes to adjust to the changing security and compliance requirements and mix of employees and external resources.

New World of Business – New Thinking in Business Management

The changes going on in the new world of business will no doubt result in new ways MBA courses will be taught in the future for how executives should manage, market, and compete in the new fast-paced global environment. Until then, executives need to step back and truly understand how these new influences impact their organization's ability to build new methods of sales, marketing, manufacturing, support, and operations to remain competitive, to grow and thrive with the fast-paced changes of today.

The bottom-line is that what got an organization to the level it is today is likely not what will help get the organization where it wants to be in the future. Tried and proven strategies that worked a decade ago need to be rethought, in some cases set aside, in determining how an organization will succeed in the new tomorrow.

CHAPTER 7: THE SHIFT FROM ACADEMIC PRACTICE TO NEW WORLD REALITY

CHAPTER 8: THE PATH FORWARD

As the analysis of changes that have occurred in the global environment over the past decade or two have been summarized in this book, along with real world examples in various industries, the question is "what should executives do to lead their organizations in this new world of seemingly constant change?"

Be Aware and Well Informed

The first piece that has been important to executives has been to be aware of the changes going on, as the pace has been so rapid, it's been hard to even keep up with the consumerization of technology, and how day to day things have been the root of many of the cultural changes going on in deep rooted enterprises.

The key for executives has been to look for threats in their business and industry, not just from traditional competitors, but from new entrants, including upstream providers that have traditionally kept in their own space but are forced to change and adapt themselves.

As has been shared from examples in this book, many of the

competitors that organizations have been facing have been from their suppliers, manufacturers, or producers. All of a sudden, organizations that have traditionally not gotten into selling directly to consumers, have the ability to do Internet marketing, social media advertising, and globally reach end customers themselves, cutting out traditional distribution and sales channels.

As a shift to a services industry marketplace, the goods and services provided are not always capital purchases, but rented or provided as a service by the week, day, or hour.

Be Fast and Nimble

Executives have found that their long term 5-year, 10-year, and beyond planning cycles have been disrupted by entrants in their line of business that are working from 6-month, 12-month, and 18-month plans. Long term plans and investments that take years or decades to play out could send the organization down a path that will limit its options as the global marketplace and consumer demands as expectations quickly change.

Manufacturers that used to spend years buying and building plant facilities are finding it difficult to compete against competitors buying excess production capacity from others and simply buying what they want, when they want it, with a much faster time to market.

Much of the watch words in the new world markets has been fast and nimble, the ability to plan, execute, and deliver in a fraction of the time than before.

Diversify

The word diversification is not purely diversifying industries but diversifying the approaches an organization has in the same or similar markets and processes. The organization may continue to "do things it always has done before" (to continue what it has been doing), but open up new and modern ways of doing the same thing, so that it has parallel paths of the same operations to build new while maintaining old.

In a manufacturing scenario, the organization may not switch all production away from existing plant facilities or stop all construction of future plant operations, but supplement production facilities with "pay as you go" manufacturing operations so that the organization splits its capacity across multiple modes of operations.

In a retail sales operation, an organization may not close down all retail operations in all markets and drastically change to an online only model, but rather build an online model in parallel to the traditional brick and mortar operation to diversity it's delivery capability without changing too much that would interrupt day to day operations.

The key has been to look to diversification and not remain stagnant for too long that would prevent the organization from being nimble and warding off competition in emerging markets and market segmentation to faster moving competitors.

Broad Set Profitability

With competition coming from venture capital funded operations to compete in some sectors of industry, an organization needs to realize it may be competing against a competitor that has no need or immediate expectation to operate profitably. If an organization wants (or needs) to compete with such enterprises, it needs to be in it for the long run, financing its operation from the profitability of other business sectors than trying to compete profitably against an organization not setup in the same manner.

This is where the diversity of service offerings can help an organization offset costs in other business areas as emerging areas grow or being forced to compete in a generally non-profitable market or industry sector.

There's also a need to change the mindset of management, investors, and shareholders that short term profitability and growth levels may be hindered as investments in long term markets, market competition areas, and opportunity space takes precedent as a deep rooted organization maintains a long term competitive market stance than focusing purely on short term profits.

Innovate with Passion

Disruptors in the global marketplace are doing so with passion, commitment, and velocity as they have nothing to lose by entering new markets and looking to chip away at the market share of traditional enterprises. Incumbents in a marketplace or those with market position need to be able to innovate and compete with the same level of passion, commitment, and velocity of change to retain their foothold in their area of business.

The challenge for deep rooted industry leaders is there has been a long-term historical predictability on profitability and business growth that changes as new entrants encroach on the market. There's a need to retain market share and business longevity in competing on a global level with new and different business models impacting the day to day operations of a business.

Assess Employee Change

As a business changes its method and mode of operations, it needs to determine whether its current workforce will be able to adapt and change as quickly as the business requires and whether those who have worked for years with the organization in one mode would even succeed and thrive in the new environment. Successful employees in an established business model may have been happy in the steady pace model of the past but be unhappy and unsuccessful in a dynamically changing new business model and environment.

Rather than retraining employees into the new model, an organization may build the new business model with new job descriptions, and hire new employees and rehire existing employees into the new model to ensure those shifting over are ready and willing to accept the way the new business is run and is ready to tackle the associated work ahead of them.

Businesses in transition are constantly assessing the fit of their personnel, and as quickly as the business changes, so must the mindset, skill, abilities, and flexibility of its workforce.

And where employees are identified as "keepers", key contributors in the new business model, leaders should present them with more than just a traditional compensation and benefits package. Today's "modern" employee needs a culture focused on employee involvement and on employee satisfaction. Some best practices include offering employees flexible, personalized work arrangements that challenge some, provide others a clear path for advancement, and still others work-life balance. And, despite technology that make digital communications easier, employees need and want collaborative communications.

Contracting for Change

Many organizations have found that as they have built a new business model, it was helpful for them to contract individuals early on to build the dynamic process and then hire and/or retrain existing employees into the new business model over time. This has allowed organizations to quickly bring on personnel, but without the commitment required for long term employment, should the new model need to be modified or changed.

When the new model achieves success, the organization can transform contractors into permanent employees, hire new employees to the new business model, and/or retrain existing employees into an already well defined and tested business model. The flexibility enables growth and change in fast paced, new, and dynamic business models as the organization adapts to variations in its business.

Enabling Technology to Solve Business Challenges

Technology has proven to be a contributing factor that helps drive these fast-paced changes. Organizations have leveraged technology solutions for communications, information sharing, and collaboration to help them solve their business challenge along the way, improving business to business, and business to customer communications.

Organizations have utilized both internal and external professionals from around the globe to extend business models beyond borders and regions in ways that were not possible prior to the readily available methods of video conferencing and instantaneous data sharing.

The power of data analytics and powerful historical information databases allows organizations the ability to analyze competitive landscapes and threats, and extend their operations into successful business models more rapidly than ever before.

Leveraging Data Analytics to be Fully Informed

Data provides information about the past and has been the method of information analysis for years. However, utilizing powerful business intelligence tools and resources, organizations can perform predictive analysis queries to project potential revenues, costs, and quantifiable market potential into the future.

Data systems provide for the integration of internal data with externally available information. Today's modernized executive should have a "dashboard" view accessible on their desktop, laptop and mobile phone of key performance indicators, internal and external information points, and measurements and assessment milestones relative to the organization's journey to change.

Wrap-Up

The global marketplace today is different than it was just two decades ago, and there's little indication that the world will revert to the way things were before. With change at our footstep and in our future, executives have the option of letting it happen around them or to thrive on this change, leveraging all that is available to build a successful business and operational model now and into the future.

This can be a scary time for executives caught flat footed and ill prepared to tackle what's ahead of them. However, for forward thinking professionals, this is a very exciting time with so much opportunity for innovation in developing new ways of doing things, being in a first mover position, and leading the marketplace and industry and never looking back.

MINI-BOOK STRATEGY SERIES

This is the seventh book in the Mini-Book Strategy Series that has taken business executives through a real time journey over the past decade on changes "cloud computing" has had with the impact of continuous technology changes in enterprises. The books have been written from meetings, interviews, and ongoing dialogs with business executives around the world, with shared best practices what organizations are doing to plan, prepare, and take advantage of the changes going on in the fast-paced global marketplace.

In order and sequence of release:

New World of I.T.

First of the series from 5+ years ago, the "New World of I.T." identified a *change* going on in the world as "cloud-technologies" were making their way into mainstream businesses, and the way organizations were going to be leveraging technologies in their businesses was about to change.

Cybersecurity: Being Cyber Aware and Cyber Safe

Second up in the series was a book on Cybersecurity and the impact that global digital security threats were going to push organizations to make rapid changes in how they store, protect, and manage their digital assets to ward off the encroachment of cyber-criminals.

Handling Electronically Stored Information (ESI) in the Era of the Cloud

The third book in the series dove into best practices how organizations are able to address the transformation to the cloud, with cybersecurity threats, and handle the security, protection, and management of digital assets wherever they reside.

Application and Datacenter Modernization

The fourth book in the series took into account that over the previous two years, organizations have extended past the early adopter phase of organizations migrating to the cloud, to the full blown transformation of organizations planning and executing on their transition of their applications and their datacenters to modern cloud platforms.

Adapting to the New World of I.T.

Firth up in the series is a title on the adaptation organizations go through as they have changed the way they're administering, managing, and maintaining new ways of cloud-based security, data storage, I.T. administration, and management.

Shifting I.T. from Technologies to a Business Services Enabler

The most recent of the series, and #6 in line addresses what happens to I.T. operations after an organization has completed their "migration" to the cloud and their modernization of I.T. This book covers how I.T. gets out of the day to day role of managing servers and datacenters, and move into a more consultative model helping their organization leverage technologies to improve the competitive advantage of the organization.

ABOUT THE AUTHORS

Rand Morimoto, Ph.D.: Dr Morimoto has a unique blend of deep technical knowledge and expertise, and an academic background in organizational behavior and organizational management. Dr Morimoto describes himself as a "tinkerer" of technologies, rolling up his sleeves and beta testing technologies months and years before the products are released to the general public. And not just one brand or solution of technologies, but his insight to what organizations want, what works, and what should be developed leads Dr Morimoto to being invited to participate in the early adopter programs of most of the key products and service providers in the industry.

Dr Morimoto is a deep-rooted academic, a lover of knowledge and information that led him to pursue his studies in an MBA program, a Doctoral program, and ultimately in the role of being on the governing board of a well-known academic institution.

Dr Morimoto blends the theory of economics and his expertise in organizational behavior and organizational management with his knowledge of the tech industry, resulting in the content highlighted in this book.

Rich Dorfman, MBA: Rich has 30+ years' experience in the information technology industry.

Rich' passions lie in business strategy, corporate culture, and how technology can help individuals and businesses. His contribution to the book focuses on targeting functional business leaders in an organization, highlighting considerations for what they need to think about and do to adjust to modern day business realities.

For the past 20+ years, Rich has managed sales, professional services operations as well as client services operations, focusing in on "New World" business development strategies and approaches, providing customized career paths, and achieving the highest-level employee and customer satisfaction.

Rich volunteers as a coach/mentor with organizations like Women in Technology, Sky's the Limit, Women in Cloud and Microsoft's Imagine Cup Competition.

Rich received his Bachelor of Arts (BA) degree at Rutgers University and has a Master of Business Administration (MBA) from Saint Mary's College, Moraga.